ROBERT LIMA

THE RITES OF STONE

THE ORLANDO PRESS

© Copyright 2010, Robert Lima

All Rights Reserved.

No part of this book may be reproduced, stored in a retrieval system, or transmitted by any means, electronic, mechanical, photocopying, recording, or otherwise, without written permission from the author.

ISBN: 978-0-940804-02-9

Published by
THE ORLANDO PRESS
485 Orlando Avenue
State College, PA 16803-3477

Acknowledgments

Some of the poems in this collection first appeared in print in the following publications:

Anthology of Contemporary Latin American Poetry
Cielo Abierto
The Forum of Phi Sigma Iota
International Poetry
Journal of General Education
The Lima Times
Nightsun
Palabras y Papel
The Penn Stater Magazine
Poema Convidado
Twelve Festival Poets Anthology

Frontispiece: No attribution. In *Fanal*, Vol. XIX, # 69 (1964), now defunct
Map of Rapa Nui by Cristián Arévalo Pakarati

Dedication

With Gratitude

To my Peruvian friend and distinguished colleague Dr. Eugenio Chang-Rodríguez

To Dr. Tom Dillehay, archaeologist and fellow Fulbrighter in Perú

To my Peruvian colleagues at *LEXIS, Revista de Literatura y Lingüística* in Lima

Frontispiece: Archaeological Map of Perú xiii

INCIDENTS OF TRAVEL TO ANCIENT ANDEAN &
PACIFIC SITES xv

Map of Rapa Nui xxxvi
       Epigraph xxxix

PART ONE

THE ANDEAN SUITE

CHANCAY 3
       Still Life 5
       Dunesaying 6
       Calendar 7
       Filaments 8

CHAVIN DE HUANTAR 9
       Chavin de Huantar 11
       Theory 13

CUSCO 15
       Sacsayhuaman 17
       Rememberers 18
       Apacheta 19
       Runner 20

GARAGAY 21
       Frieze 23

HUANCAYO ALTO - YANGAS 25
       Huancayo Alto - Yangas 27

HUARAZ	29
Monoliths	31
Fardo	33
Participants	34
KOTOSH	35
Kotosh	37
LAMBAYEQUE	39
Túcume Viejo	41
MACHU PICCHU	43
Intihuatana	45
Huayna Picchu	46
Tamputtoco	47
MOCHE - MOCHICA	49
Mythos	51
Virú	52
Palace	53
Omission	54
Huaca del Dragón	55
Cerro Blanco	56
Pieces	57
NAZCA	59
Markers	61
Designation	62
OLLANTAYTAMBO	63
Remnants	65
Legend	66

PACHACAMAC 67
                Precincts of the God 69
                Yuncas Deity 72

PAÑAMARCA 73
                Huaca 75
                Petrography 76

PARAMONGA 77
                Citadel 79

PURUCHUCO 81
                Domain 83

SECHIN 85
                Glyphs 87
                Decapitation 88

SILLUSTANI 89
                Death Height 91
                Chullpas 93

TIAWANAKU 95
                Portal Of The Sun 97
                Template 98

PART TWO

THE PACIFIC SUITE

RAPA NUI 101
                        Settlement Pattern 103
                        Moai 105
                        Nightfall............................ 108
                        The Loss 109
                        Hollowness 110
                        Restoration 111
                        Make Make 112
                        Metamorphosis..................... 113
                        Illumination........................ 114
About the Author 115

TABLE OF ILLUSTRATIONS

Front Cover: Machu Picchu, Perú

Frontispiece: Archaeological Map of Perú xiii

Map of Rapa Nui xxxvi

CHANCAY: Statuette of a female deity 3

CHAVIN DE HUANTAR: Lanzón 9

CUSCO: Twelve-angled Inka Stone & Wall 15

GARAGAY: Frieze 21

HUANCAYO ALTO: Lake and Mountain with Glacier 25

HUARAZ: Statue of Recuay Warrior 29

KOTOSH: Temple of the Crossed Hands 35

LAMBAYEQUE: Adobe Pyramid of Túcume Viejo 39

MOCHE-MOCHICA: Huaca del Dragón or Huaca Arco Iris 49

NAZCA: Nazca Monkey and Hummingbird 59

OLLANTAYTAMBO: Massive Granite Monolithic Walls 63

PACHACAMAC: Effigy of the god Pachacamac 67

PAÑAMARCA: Mural with Anthro-Zoomorphic & Other Images 73

PARAMONGA: Chimú Fortress 77

PURUCHUCO: Palace Site... 81

SECHIN: Wall Depicting Severed Heads............................... 85

SILLUSTANI: Funerary Chullpa 89

TIAWANAKU: Portrait of Sun God Inti 95

RAPA NUI: Recumbent Moai.. 101

Back Cover: Rapa Nui Moai at sunset

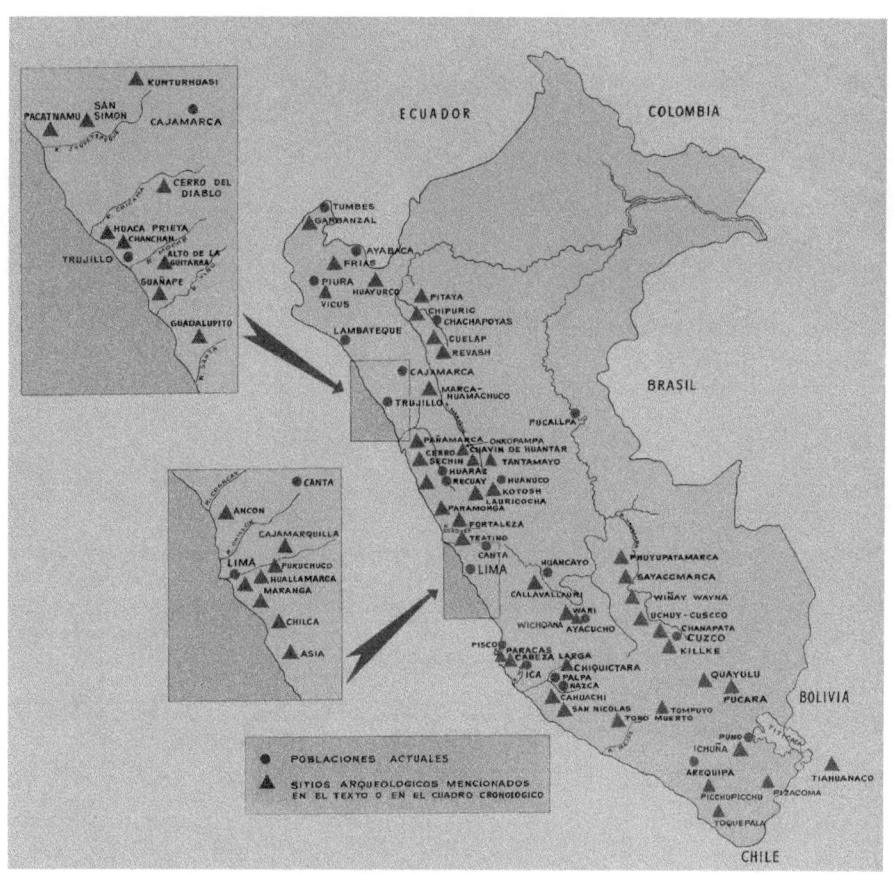

Archaeological Map of Perú

INCIDENTS OF TRAVEL TO ANCIENT ANDEAN & PACIFIC SITES

During my stay in Perú as a Senior Fulbright Fellow, I took every opportunity when not teaching or doing poetry readings in the capital to visit archaeological sites throughout the length and breadth of the Andean nation. My travels took me from the lowlands of the coastal desert to mountain peaks, and into the lush jungle; from the areas around colonial Trujillo and Lambayeque in the north, into Machu Picchu and Puno on Lake Titicaca in the interior, to Nazca and Paracas in the south. And many points in between. The sites I encountered are too numerous to count and the cultural variety they represent extremely complex, ranging back in time to thousands of years B.C.E. and forward to the pre-Conquest Inkas.

While in Lima, I visited four of its museums. The Museo Nacional de Antropología y Arqueología del Perú, the Museo Oro del Perú, the Japanese-Peruvian family-owned Museo Amano de Textiles, and another private collection, the Museo Arqueológico Rafael Larco Herrera, popularly known as the Museo Erótico. The first has the most and best selection of Peruvian antiquities, covering all periods—from lithic beginnings to the Inka hegemony; there I was able to plot out the routes to the sites I wanted to visit. The Museo del Oro, true to its name, contains gold crafts from many indigenous peoples, ranging from filigree work to hammered sheets, from jewelry to regal accouterments: breast plates, headdresses, ceremonial weaponry, body adornments, figurines such as *tumis* (said to be ceremonial knives), and grave goods in the precious metal that the museum highlights. The third collection contains examples of the textile artistry of early Peruvians collected by a prominent family. The fourth museum houses an amazing collection of erotic materials featuring heterosexual, homosexual and egosexual activities in very explicit depictions on ceramic pots and statuary from throughout the country's areas and cultures. Only adults are permitted entry and, for the longest time, only males. I suppose the exclusion made it easier for men to study the penis lengths, masturbatory techniques, coital positions, bestiality, and related practices (as of monkeys) that the exhibits depicted. Now women are allowed to see holdings which to modern eyes are explicitly pornographic but to pre-Christian viewers were matter-of-fact representations of their unbridled human sexuality. The fecundity of human, animal and plant life has always been a major concern of ancient peoples; in Perú, they described it visually in their arts and crafts.

These and other museum experiences extended throughout my nearly year-long stay in the country, as did my trips to archaeological sites. My first such visit to a *huaca*, as pyramids in Perú are called, was in the San Isidro section of Lima where I was staying. Although small, Huaca Huallamarca, named after the Huallas people who erected it, is almost 100 feet in height and a city-block square. Dating from 100 B.C.E., it is a triple truncated temple faced with adobe bricks in the form of grains of maize. Having been used by later groups, there is evidence of potsherds from other cultures. A small museum adjacent to the *huaca* features the mummified remains of a *curaca*, a chieftan, in an elaborate shroud, which was covered in a mantle of toucan and parrot feathers; his staff of authority and vessels containing food for the afterlife accompany the remains. The *huaca* is impressive in its architecture and has been perfectly preserved through careful tending and restoration. I was to find that such attention to antiquities typified not only the professional archaeologist's attitude but also that of the populace at large throughout Perú, perhaps because the pyramids and other ancient sites were still thought of as dwellings of the gods. Christianity may be the official religion of the country but the old beliefs are still extant.

Not as close but at a distance of 32 kilometers sufficiently nearby to go by bus was the site known as Pachacamac. This large complex was next to the Pacific Ocean and parapets on its structures provided exceptional views of sand and sea. Not unlike many Roman cities,

Pachacamac was sited by the water both for aesthetic and strategic reasons. Its name, rather appropriate to its setting, is composed of "pacha" (meaning earth) and "camaq" (meaning embrace), thus "the one that dominates the earth." Pachacamac, as the name is now written, was the Huari God of Creation.

Along broad avenues and narrow alleys, remnants of large adobe buildings evidenced the past importance of the place. It was a 4th century B.C.E. Huari center first, seat of an Oracle of great prestige, and then upon falling to the Inka, became the largest of their coastal cities. The highest point is atop the Inka Temple of the Sun, which at nearly 300 feet served as the placement for the great disk that reflected the rays of the solar deity for long distances along sea, desert and mountain. Among other impressive buildings is the Mamacuna Temple, dubbed "Temple of the Virgins," with its numerous trapezoidal doorways and windows, Inka architectural hallmarks. The vast building and its courtyard is believed to have served the young women as a sacred precinct and a residence before entering the royal household as concubines.

Taken by its setting, the magnitude of the complex, and its importance as a center of two religious traditions, it was at Pachacamac that I began writing the poems that would in time become *The Rites of Stone*, a work that encompasses the majority of sites I visited near Lima, across the country, and in Bolivia.

North of the capital lay the town of Chancay. The thirty-seven kilometers from the capital were easily overcome by taking a *colectivo*, a shared taxi that departed when full. Such cabs ranged far and wide along the Pan American Highway, the principal coastal artery, some making short hops and returning to Lima within hours, others taking passengers to very distant points, not making the trek back for several days. With some of the highest dunes in the world alongside the highway, it was often necessary to wait for hours for road crews to clear the road. At other times, the trip would be interrupted at police or military checkpoints.

Once in Chancay, I walked across the highway through a flat, desolate landscape. Eventually, I reached my destination. This was the burial site of the ancients who had pursued lives before the coming of the Spanish. There were no markers at the necropolis. But the site was littered with thousands of shards, remnants of the pottery, statuary and other burial goods of the Chancay Culture. The place had been defiled by *huaqueros*, the Peruvian term for grave robbers, and archaeologists had abandoned it as worthless for methodical study. To me, however, the solitude it offered and the evidence of past lives it contained provided me with resources for my poetry. I sat among broken skulls and other bones as I wrote of what I saw around me and what I intuited.

When I got up to leave, and only then, three Indian women in traditional dress approached me. They unburdened themselves of the shawls across their backs and spread them on the sand; before me lay objects the like of which I had seen only in museums! There were complete pots and beautifully molded statues bearing the distinctive black markings on an off-white slip of the Chancay style; there were also fascinating wooden figurines with mother-of-pearl eyes; there were small boxes, each with its own intricately carved pattern; there were fragments of burial cloths; there were doll-like "poppets" sewn together in over-the-shoulder padded carriers ... They were all offered to me for sale. Although I knew I could not take them out of the country, I decided to help the local economy by purchasing several small pieces; at least they would be with me during the rest of my stay in Perú.

I returned to the town to get a *colectivo* back to Lima and while waiting in the small plaza I was approached by a policeman. I figured that, like the three women, he had been watching me; I sensed that he knew I had made a purchase and that he was about to confiscate my goods and, perhaps, throw me in jail. But I was wrong on the last two. With a knowing smile, he invited me to his house, promising a surprise. We sat in his livingroom and soon his wife offered us coffee; a short time later, his son appeared bearing packages wrapped in newspaper. My host opened these carefully and, with a great dramatic flair, placed the content of each before me. If I had marveled at the offerings of the three women, the policeman's haul flabbergasted me. He had a collection of perfect pots and statues, several two feet in height. His was a real treasure for it included gold and beaded jewelry! Again, I was offered the pieces. Under the circumstances, I was afraid to leave without making a purchase, concerned that my previous fears might come true. And so I bought one of the pots and a small ceramic statue, protesting that I could not afford to spend any more *Soles,* Perú's monetary units, if I was to have enough to return to Lima. He walked me to the plaza and bid me *adios* as I boarded my taxi; I was nonetheless apprehensive—he could still confiscate my goods and put me in the local hoosegow. I did not feel safe until the cab left the town limits. Although I returned to the necropolis on two other occasions, I was careful to get off on the highway rather than in town. Just in case ...

At other times, I traveled beyond the environs of Lima. One extended trip took me to the north coastal city of Trujillo, founded in 1535 and named by Francisco Pizarro after his place of origin in Spain. Although the rich colonial heritage is everywhere—in plazas, churches, municipal buildings, palaces, private homes—I went there to visit the archaeological sites within its sphere.

Trujillo attracts many tourists because it is one of the most important centers for the first-hand study of Peruvian archaeology. Within a few kilometers of the city are the extensive ruins of Chan Chan, the once magnificent adobe metropolis which was the seat of the great Chimú Empire until it was conquered by the Inkas and abandoned. Also close by are the imposing Huaca del Dragón or Arco Iris, a ramped pyramid distinguished by its anthropomorphic friezes, the Sol and Luna pyramid complex, Huaca Esmeralda, with adobe decorations similar to those at Chan Chan, and Templo de los Reyes, with its biped figures and feline heads.

But Trujillo itself has an archaeological attraction which merits the attention of tourist and researcher alike. Its location gives it a rather low profile, however, and an effort is required to detect it, if a small one.

En route to Chan Chan and Huaca del Dragón is the junction of the road to Huanchaco and the Pan-American Highway; at the delta stands the Grifo Cassinelli. If you're driving, stop; if you're on a *colectivo* or a mini-carrier, known as *micro*, ask to be let off; if on foot, take off your backpack. You've arrived at *the* destination.

Stroll into the office of the petrol station and ask to see the *huacos*, as the ceramic artefacts found in *huacas* (pyramids) are called. The woman behind the counter will ask for 60 Soles (later Intis, now Nuevos Soles), upon payment of which you'll be escorted through yet another office. This inner room is filled with large ceramic pieces for the most part, but it is not what one has come to see primarily, it is only one of several "overflow" areas. The guide then takes you through a door that leads underground, beneath the petrol station.

When the lights are turned on at the foot of the stairs, you enter a medium-sized room and are confronted by the more than 2,000 stunning pieces in stone, clay, bone, wood, metal, precious stones and cloth that comprise the viewable collection of the Museo Arqueológico "José Cassinelli Mazzei."

Possibly the least-known of the Peruvian private collections open to the public, it is one of the most admirable in the quality and scope of its holdings. The Cassinelli Museum houses pieces from early Andean cultures—Chavín, Recuay, Virús, Mochica, Nazca, Tiawanaku, Huari, Chimú–to the Inka hegemony, including some of the most unusual and finest examples of each of these cultures.

Every kind of object associated with the pre-Hispanic cultures of Peru can be seen, from the representational to the abstract. Among the curiosities are items concerned with witchcraft, medicine, sexual relations, fishing, hunting, business, housing, and war. Lifestyles and customs are amply manifested in a variety of techniques.

Sr. Cassinelli began collecting *huacos* early on, first with the curiosity of the youngster and later with the passion of a man who wished to preserve part of the nation's patrimony. The vault-like room beneath the petrol station provided the security and space requisite for his holdings. But as the assemblage of artifacts grew, the space became inadequate; many fine pieces had to be stored away in crates and could not be produced for examination except with difficulty. The situation has worsened over the years.

It was Sr. Cassinelli's dream to erect a building adjacent to the *grifo*, on land he had already bought, and install his collection therein. The dream progressed to the point where architect's renderings had been submitted for approval but was stymied on the matter of financing. When I visited, he was looking for the assistance of an individual, a group, or a foundation to build the two-story structure. I was so taken by the collection, little known outside the area, and its "secret" location that I published an article, "Petrol Isn't All That's Underground," in *The Lima Times* to promote it throughout greater Perú.

If Sr. Cassinelli's hopes materialize, Trujillo will gain an impressive cultural center of the magnitude of the Bruning Museum in Lambayeque. In the meantime, the Grifo Cassinelli continues to provide a quaint underground setting for some of the best *huacos* in Perú. The experience of a visit should not be missed.

From the Grifo Cassinelli I went to the nearby Huaca del Dragón, so-called because of the zoomorphic friezes that adorn its walls, although another repeated motif, a series of arched lines above a stylized centipede resembling a rainbow, have also given it the name Huaca Arco Iris. Being a terraced pyramid with successively receding levels, the structure is not unlike an Assyro-Babylonian ziggurat.

My third visit in the vicinity was to Chan Chan, whose name means Sun, twice over. The largest adobe city in the world—its central area alone covers almost two miles, its population being

50,000 in antiquity—the seaside metropolis first thrived from 200 B.C.E. to 800 C.E. under its founders, the Mochica or Moche, who developed an extensive underground water supply and sewage system. The capital of the empire and its holdings, which reached as far north as Tumbes, near the border with present-day Ecuador, and southward to Supe, then passed into the control of another remarkable people, the Chimú.

Alone at the site, except for the gatekeeper, I walked for hours through the grid-like sectors of the vast city. Everywhere were rectangular units of varying size—temples, palaces, courtyards, baths, gardens, terraces and platforms—surrounded by well-preserved adobe walls reaching great heights. Everywhere too walls were embellished with embossed geometric and zoomorphic images similar to those at the Huaca del Dragón but here the cormorant, a dark-plumed, web-footed marine diving bird, was the most common. When there was a break in the bastions, the Pacific Ocean was clearly visible and I could image ancient mariners astride their *caballitos de totora*, reed bundles fastened with ropes, such as those depicted on their pottery, fishing those waters along with cormorants.

The Mochica and their cultural inheritors, the Chimú, were also exceptional portrayers of every aspect of their lives, particularly in the countless ceramics that depict facial expressions, medical procedures, and daily endeavors on all levels of their societies, including sexual practices. I had seen huge numbers of their ceramics in museums in Lima and elsewhere; no two were alike. So numerous are they, that museums house the majority of their holdings in storage areas filled with floor-to-ceiling racks; fortunately, they are made accessible to professionals.

There are other important archaeological sites of the Moche-area peoples on the near outskirts of Trujillo. Accompanied by a local guide, we went to her house to meet her brother, who would be our driver. He seemed a likable fellow but when I entered the car I noticed that he had placed a machete next to him on the front seat, "in case we meet *huaqueros*" (graverobbers), he explained. I wondered if brother and sister formed a "get the tourist" combo and I was their intended victim. Nonetheless, I ventured, if uneasily, to the arid plain that housed two pyramids, Huaca del Sol and Huaca de la Luna. The first, like its better-known cousin in Mexico, is huge. Both in height and girth it rivals the Teotihuacan pyramid, but unlike that stone structure the adobe of which it is built is highly eroded. Accompanied by my guide (her brother, machete in hand, stayed at the bottom), I climbed its precarious levels to a height, everywhere seeing the holes *huaqueros* had made in their illegal search for gold artefacts. The apex permitted a rewarding view of its smaller sister pyramid and of the entire Moche valley. We then traveled to Virú and yet another, if smaller *huaca*, this time accompanied by the machete-wielder because there were men at the top. But they too were tourists. Afterwards, we returned to the city, where my guide's mother treated us to refreshments while her brother retired the ominous machete. I returned to my hotel grateful that the day had passed without incident.

Back in Lima, I would prepare for four of the most important trips I was to undertake. Each required a journey from the capital by air. The first of these was to Huaraz, a small city in the midst of the Callejón de Huaylas, a valley between the Cordillera Blanca and the Cordillera Negra, mountain ranges in central Peru. It was a means to an end, the jumping off place for Chavín de Huantar, site of one of the primal cultures of the entire Andes region.

I arranged to join a group of locals heading for Chavín the morning after my arrival. I was picked up at my hotel and driven to the meeting point, where I boarded a minivan. A few moments later, the man with whom I had contracted for the trip entered to introduce the driver—a boy of about fourteen! We were told that he was the best driver on the route and the hazardous journey of four hours through precipice-lined, two-way mountain "roads" proved him right. Not once were all four wheels over the chasms, one or two a lot, causing passengers to shift to the opposite side as if in a yawing yacht. It was the most memorable ride I've ever endured, outstripping even those in Mexican buses with macho drivers trying to impress the ubiquitous girlfriend on the front seat. Too young to have a female companion, at least on the van, our teenager was serious and wholly committed to driving, no matter what it took to get us to our exotic destination.

We arrived in front of the great archaeological site and I soon purchased an entry ticket. I entered first the "plaza" of the building that is called "El Castillo" (castle), with its highly stylized tenon heads protruding from the walls. These images, as well as bas-reliefs incised on friezes, are anthropomorphic and zoomorphic, often depicting monstrous beings, condors, and pumas, at other times showing abstract motifs. But the principal image at Chavín is found within the dark innards of the Castillo. It is called "El Lanzón" for it resembles a massive lance hurled into the floor of the structure, where it stands as one of the strangest of sculptures in Perú or elsewhere. Its vertical axis is set at the center of a cruciform, the fifteen-feet high granite monolith embedded into floor and ceiling. In its placement and immobility, it may actualize Chavín as the "navel of the world," a concept found in many antique societies.

The stela is carved into a series of intertwining spirals that represent hair or a headdress but the most singular feature is the grinning mouth out of whose upper reaches extend large lateral fangs. It is polymorphous in its integration of serpent and jaguar aspects. Prismic in form, the "Lanzón" can be viewed from either of its sides; no matter the perspective, the profile is intimidating. The same can be said of another interpretation of the idol, that image on a flat stone, embellished with more realistic-looking snakes and clawed feet, that has come to be known as the Raimondi Stela, after its discoverer.

Together, the powerful visual images of Chavín de Huantar—the formal curvilinear and abstract patterns on monochrome vases, the Raimondi Stela, the fanged felines, the embedded heads, and, most notably, the ferocious "Lanzón"—were to reach all areas of Perú and to permeate Andean art for centuries, stretching as far as Colombia's

San Agustín archaeological site, with its ferocious stelae and statuary.

My second destination lay in the jungle and to get to it I had to first reach Cusco, once the capital of the Inkas. Cusco is the gateway to Machu Picchu. As Chavín de Huantar is the primal culture of northern and central Perú, so Cusco is the pivotal site for Inka civilization, for as the early Spanish historians of the region were told, the city was founded by the legendary Manco Capac. It is thus the center of the four regions of what was to become the Inka Empire, that peoples' own "Navel of the World."

I flew to Cusco on AeroPeru, spending a night in the Inka capital at a small establishment housed within massive Inka stone walls "so closely fitted that a knife blade could not penetrate the seams." I would soon be able to verify the claim that I had come across so often. I was strangely tired upon arrival. One acclimates to the altitude by walking slowly to one's room after registering, imbibing the complimentary coca tea, and taking a siesta. If during the rite of passage one sees images of Inka warriors on the massive walls, all the better.

Throughout the city, as at my inn, one encounters the remnants of buildings from pre-Conquest times, most notably the foundation on which the Catholic cathedral is erected (since antiquity, new religions superimposed their temples over those of the vanquished). The city itself is a vast museum of such adaptations to modern needs, from housing to shops, including numerous boutique-sized places selling hand-carved masks, others offering Inka artefacts or colonial furniture.

Having walked the narrow cobbled streets off the central plaza, I came across a strange establishment to find in Cusco, the American Bar, whose clientele included Gary Trudeau, the creator of the Doonesbury cartoons. But the celebrity was rather morose and had little to say. At his table I met expatriates from several nations and one of them, an American who had "gone native," offered a variety of Inka artefacts for sale. Again, anxious to help support the locals, even if an American abroad, I accompanied him to his quarters, where I was treated to another great display of archaeological items. The country, it seemed, was full of such treasures in private hands. I bought several remnants of burial cloths; my room back in Lima still had space for a few such acquisitions.

I also took an excursion by taxi to outlying Inka sites. These included Sacsayhuaman (variant Sacsahuamán), the magnificent fortress made of huge stone blocks in a zigzag pattern that looms over Cusco as its guardian; it is also the setting for the yearly Inti Raymi festival...celebrated on June 24th in honor of the Sun. Beyond, lay Kenko, with the striking "Puma Stone" carved into passages, canals, houses, stairs and pumas (a similar but smaller stone is at Saihuite); and Tambo Machay, with its Inka bath, both on the road to the citadel above Pisac. Thereafter, I proceeded first to Moray, with its amazing upside-down, truncated conical terraces, a great agricultural earthworks at a depth of over three hundred feet, which was irrigated in Inca times by aqueducts; then it was on to Ollantaytambo, the extensive hillside ruins most noted for the fortress with its vertical terraces atop of which six monoliths guard the Temple of the Sun.

The next day required an early rising to make the train to Machu Picchu. The start of the journey is of particular interest to railroad buffs because the train must negotiate numerous switchbacks as it climbs the heights surrounding the city. Once these have been accomplished, the locomotive chugs on narrow-gauge tracks, frequently along river's edge. Nature is magnificent viewed from the train. But there are more intrepid travelers who choose to make the secular pilgrimage to Machu Picchu on foot, trekking for four days through a panorama of mountain, river, jungle that takes the hiker to other Inka sites as well.

There is no question that Machu Picchu has, in the realtor's phrase, "Location, location, location!" I have been to many exotic locales across the globe but none can match the so-called "lost city of the Inkas." Machu Picchu ("Old Peak," in Quechua) has a setting that takes the breath away, tucked on a tight plateau between towering peaks, high above the Urubamba River, surrounded by lush vegetation. In the early morning hours it is frequently shrouded by fog and if it weren't in Perú, it might be mistaken for the Shangri-La in James Hilton's *Lost Horizon*. Like that fictional city, Machu Picchu is so difficult to find that it was not until 1911 that Hiram Bingham discovered the site for the West (the locals knew of it all along). The seclusion and grandeur of the site can be compared only to that of Petra, the hidden 4th century B.C.E. "rose-red city" of the Nabateans, in present-day Jordan.

Machu Picchu may or may not be as old as Petra but it is certainly much older than the Inka. Although touted as built by the last great civilization of the Andes before the conquest by Pizarro, the complex of buildings and agricultural terraces was erected long before by an unknown culture, as evidenced by the irregular stones that serve as foundations, and refurbished by the Inka with their massive, tightly fitted blocks and trapezoidal gateways. And while Petra was captured by the Romans in 106 C.E., Machu Picchu was never conquered by the Spanish.

The heights of Machu Picchu, as the Chilean Pablo Neruda titled his famed collection of poems, are reached by an autobus that meets the train at Santa Ana. Upon entering the main portal, it is seen that the site houses a wide variety of structures largely erected on either side of the esplanade central to the site, the more impressive being: a series of structures along the terraces and an observation hut from which the entire site can be appreciated; a building with three extant trapezoidal windows that sits above a series of terraces; a three-walled rectangular structure with many niches and an altar stone; a tower with curved and inclined walls abuts a rectangular bastion and, at its base, a man-made incursion into the natural rock to serve, it is said, as a burial chamber (although it may have functioned as an oracular center, as at Delphi); the sides of a staircase serve as a conduit for water falling into collecting areas; numerous small houses or administrative centers; and, at the highest point of the built-up area, the Intihuatana, whose name means "the hitching post of the Sun," an irregularly carved block of granite whose apex is prism-shaped and may have been the ceremonial center of the complex. The entire site is overseen by the hulking breadloaf-like mass of Huayna Picchu ("Young Peak"), where smaller ruins can be accessed upon a precipitous climb that provides yet another amazing view of the Machu Picchu site.

Returning by train to Cusco, I traveled south to Pucara and Sillustani, using Puno as my base. Preparations were underway for the city's festival of La Diablada, a celebration of the defeat of the Devil and his cohorts by St. Michael and his Archangels held yearly. I took the opportunity when invited to don a devil mask and dance with the men, who for the most part were thoroughly enjoying their intoxication via *chicha* (fermented maize drink) or *aguardiente* ("white lightning"); nobody bothered with brewery-styled beer. Having been invited to drink of each (it would have been unthinkable to have abstained), I retired to my quarters to recuperate for the next morning's trek. A headache notwithstanding, I set out for Sillustani, there to see the *chullpas*. These are massive stone structures several stories high in which ancient peoples placed the dead in a sitting position against the circular walls. Years later, when I visited *brochs* in Scotland and *nuraghi* in Sardinia, they reminded me of the strange Peruvian towers near Lake Titicaca.

The third excursion was to Nazca, site of the enigmatic lines on the several *pampas* that have haunted the minds of many and caused one, the mathematician Maria Reiche, to devote most of her life to their care and attempted decipherment. It was at the Hotel Turistas that I stayed on the day before flying over the lines and it was there that I met Ms Reiche and had occasion to listen to her fascinating interpretation of the immense drawings. I was better prepared because of her instruction when I flew over them but that didn't prevent my feeling a great awe at the minds that had envisioned the drawings or the hands that had executed them on the earth of the pampas. Whatever the reason behind their creation, the massive spiral-tailed monkey, spider, hummingbird, and geometric patterns stun one into silence at the genius that brought them into being. Their meaning may never be known but these images forever impress themselves on the minds of any who have seen them in person. The Nazca lines are truly worthy of the oft-abused word "Awesome!"

When I completed the semester of teaching and doing poetry readings in Lima, I set out for my fourth major destination. This was in Bolivia, off the shores of Lake Titicaca, the highest navigable body of water in the world. Arriving in La Paz, the capital, I settled into a hotel and began the process of becoming acclimated to the altitude; by evening I'd managed to feel relatively sound and ventured to conquer the several sloping streets that mark the city's contours. I soon came upon the so-called Witches Market, where among hundreds of items, fetuses of llamas and other animals are sold as good luck charms, particularly to place in the cornerstones of new buildings and homes. Acquiring a shiny glass eye as protection from any evil eye that might be cast my way, I set out to eat (at a German restaurant) and then I retired to get ready for my early morning departure.

Tiawanaku (variant Tiahuanaco) is on the southern shore of the great lake. It was there and on the sacred islands of the Sun and the Moon in the lake that the pantheon of the gods of that culture had its origin and it was from this center that the civilization bearing its name was to spread through Bolivia, Perú, northern Chile, and Ecuador.

The site is imposing. Rather than a city, Tiawanaku was a ceremonial center. Tradition has it that this was the home of Viracocha, the creator god and it may be his image centered atop The Gateway of the Sun (Inti), a monolithic portal that has come to be, along with Machu Picchu, the defining achievement of Andean archaeology. The central figure is holding a staff or sceptre in each hand; he looks out somberly, his head, surrounded by emanations that may be a stylized sunburst or a feathered headdress, being in higher relief than the rest of his body. Positioned on high, the god or ruler that the image represents is indeed arresting. His superior status is enhanced by the rows of attendant figures, forty-eight in all—first and third rows are human, second row are condor-masked, each carrying a staff, and all have condor wings. Curiously, the hands of all figures show only the thumb and three fingers. Below is a frieze that alternates a linear motif with the face of the god or ruler. In contrast, the Gateway of the Moon is smaller and unadorned, although it too is made of a single stone.

The portal stands at one edge of a megalithic enclosure (Calasasaya) that formed part of the walls of a stepped-pyramid (Acapana). Off the Calasasaya is the large rectangular sunken plaza, six steps below, its walls encrusted with tenoned heads, as at Chavín de Huantar (some label them trophy heads); it is an open-air space, probably ceremonial in nature, in which monoliths of different heights feature stylized human figures and animals, as well as pictographs. In its present state of reconstruction, the space resembles a Zen garden. Such monolithic sculptures have given rise to the theory that they are related to the gigantic figures on Rapa Nui (Easter Island). They have in common massive size, sculpting of a single stone block, a topknot, an unexpressive frontal stare, arms across the chest or stomach (sometimes holding a container; an offering, perhaps?). Similar figures are found in San Agustín, Colombia and in the Mapuche areas of Chile.

Mine had been a journey that had taken me to nearly all the principal sites of ancient civilizations in Perú (Sipán had not yet been discovered) and Bolivia. In Perú, among others, I had covered the major central coastal sites of Pachacamac, Chancay, Garagay (fierce zoomorphic friezes that recall Chavín), had been as far north as Lambayeque, Chiclayo and Trujillo, visiting the Paramonga fortress, Puruchuco, Chan Chan, Huaca del Sol, Cerro Sechín (with its monoliths of fierce warriors and their trophy heads), and as far south as Arequipa, viewing ruins at Paracas, Ica, Tambo Colorado and the incredible Nazca Lines; in the interior, I had been to Chavín de Huantar (housing the Lanzón), Kotosh (with its mysterious folded arms frieze), Machu Picchu (twice), Cusco, Ollantaytambo, Tambo Machay, Yucay, Pisac, Sacsayhuaman, Puno, Pucara and Sillustani; in Bolivia, to Lake Titicaca and Tiawanaku.

It made sense to next pursue the cultures of northern Chile and after a brief stay in Santiago, the capital, I headed to the Atacama Desert, a vast and very arid region that contains Inka and pre-Inkaic ruins, such as at Quitor, Zapar and Lasana, and cemeteries with mummies wrapped in *fardos* (funerary bundles) still in situ. In the vicinity of Pintados, there are hundreds of geoglyphs of unknown origin featuring fauna, humans and abstract geometric patterns. But the most outsized of all is the so-called Atacama Giant, at 304 feet in height, with a huge width enhanced by extended arms, the humanoid figure traced on the dune is the largest such representation in the world.

Returning to Santiago de Chile, I visited two impressive collections at the Natural History Museum and the Pre-Colombian Museum, seeing the surprising wooden effigies of the Mapuche culture, with their Stoic stylized features, arms folded below the chest, and topknots, all reminiscent of the Tiawanaku statuary. And of the Moai on Rapa Nui, with their *pukao*, the red scoria topknots.

My next stop would be that isolated Pacific island, known also as Easter Island and Isla de Pascuas (after the day of its discovery by the Dutch in 1722), where I would gauge for myself the probable relationship of the massive stone figures there to the monoliths at Tiawanaku and the wooden counterparts of the Mapuche.

Just as Cusco was held by the Inka to be "The Navel of the World," so too is Rapa Nui seen as the source of life in its tradition, "Te Pito o Te Henua" in the native language. The island has been a Chilean possession since 1888. Located 2,300 miles from the South American continent and 1,289 miles from Pitcairn Island, its nearest inhabited Pacific neighbor, it is one of the most isolated places in the world. To reach it required a five-hour flight from Santiago into Mataveri Airport on the military base at Hanga Roa, the only major population center, located on the western side of the triangular island.

I was met at the terminal with a lei in the traditional Polynesian welcome and driven to the nearby Ota'i Hotel, a charming family-run group of one-story buildings around a garden courtyard with a swimming pool. I would spend six nights in its comfortable precincts and take most of my meals there; from the Ota'i I walked several times to the Father Sebastian Englert Archaeological Museum, founded by the Bavarian priest who spent much of his life on Rapa Nui. The museum houses a relic of great importance found in 1978—a white coral "eye" that had belonged in the empty eye-socket of a Moai, evidence that at one time the statues, now without "eyes," could "see."

The sights of Rapa Nui should be experienced in a relaxed, unhurried way, and I took my time in seeing each area fully and sitting among its riches to write about what I observed.

First, I visited Tahai, Vai Uri and Ko Te Riku, three *ahu*, platforms that the archaeologist William Molloy had re-erected in 1968, supporting Moai that face inland, as do all the statues. The vicinity also offered the opportunity to view a *hare paenga*, the foundation of a boat-shaped dwelling, and to enter a habitation cave, of which there are many examples on the island, along with lava tubes that show signs of human visitation in antiquity. Some have suggested that these earthen interiors served as places of refuge during times of conflict based on evidence of hearths, pottery shards, paintings and, in some, human remains within their confines.

Rapa Nui has three major volcanoes, one at each vertex of the triangle. There are numerous other volcanic cones of smaller size. But Rano Raraku is the site where most of the island's Moai were quarried; some lay on its slopes half-finished while others are in situ on the rockface, as if attempting to emerge from its bondage as is the case with the largest Moai of all. The interior of the volcanic cone is now a lake bounded by totora reeds and still more statues. It was from this site that, somehow, the massive monoliths were moved to their platforms throughout Rapa Nui. How that was achieved remains an enigma despite the efforts of Thor Heyerdahl and others to device a practical method to account for such a logistical achievement. Island tradition has it that the monoliths "walked" to their destinations.

The Poike Peninsula, on the island's easternmost extension, contains many *ahu*, including Hanga Poukura, Ahu Vaihu, where eight toppled Moai are face down with their topknots scattered on the ground, and Ahu Hanga Te Tenga site of the largest Moai in the area. The environs are also replete with statues and ancient settlements. At Ahu Tongariki is an array of fifteen Moai re-erected by Chilean archaeologists; at Ahu Te Pito Kura lies the enormous statue known as Paro, last-known to be toppled from its *ahu*, and a stone, that as legend has it, is the actual Navel of the World. Following the coast north, the beautiful palm-laden beach at Anakena provides the background to the re-erected Moai of Ahu Naunau.

Arriving at Vinapu on the southeastern part of the island, I saw the perfectly-fitted stones of Ahu Tahiri, very reminiscent of the famed Inka walls in Cusco and elsewhere throughout the continental empire. Nearby, at Maunga Orito, obsidian shards, the result of volcanic eruptions, had provided the ancient peoples with the material for spear points, knives, and other war and household implements. Then it was off to Huri a Urenga to view another re-erected Moai, this one distinguished by its four hands across its front, and on to Ahu Akivi, which, unlike the majority of *ahu* situated along the coasts, stands inland. At Puna Pau, it was evident that the small volcanic crater was the quarry for the *pukao*, the red-stone topknots that sat atop each Moai. At Ahu Tepeu I saw the largest of the island's *hare paenga*, the remnants of another boat-shaped house.

My last full day on Rapa Nui began very early in order to meet the rising sun atop Rano Kau, the extinct volcanic peak at the southwesternmost point of the island. It was there that early peoples built the ceremonial center of Orongo, poised between the lake in the crater's interior and imposing cliffs overlooking three small *motu*, islets off the peninsula. Motu Kao Kao, Motu Iti and Motu Nui were the focus of the so-called Birdman Cult, which is part of the religion in which Make Make is the creator god, said to have followed that of the Moai at some undefined period of time. Evidence of the importance of this later cult can be seen throughout Orongo in the petroglyphs and carved stones depicting Make Make and the half-bird, half-man. Tradition has it that the people gathered at Orongo when it was time to welcome the Birdman, the winner of a yearly competition that consisted of diving from the cliff, swimming out to the bird sanctuary on one of the *motu*, locating the first of the eggs laid by the terns, swimming back to the cliff and climbing its sheer face. Upon achieving this multiple feat, he would present the unsullied trophy to the ruler, who would vest the winner as the new Birdman. Descending from Orongo, I visited Ana Kai Tangata, a cave replete with beautifully-executed paintings of sooty terns so important to the ritual life at Orongo. A boat ride through choppy waters gave me the opportunity to sail around the *motu* of the Birdman but the sea's turbulence prevented a planned landing on any of the three islets. Nonetheless, I could observe closely their craggy geology and view the daunting heights of the sheer cliffs across from them, even more so as the boat approached their base. The achievement of all who undertook to compete for the honor of being vested as the Birdman could now be appreciated not only as an incredible physical feat but also as a measure of the human spirit's ability to surpass apparent limitations.

    The heights of Orongo and its great rite behind me, I returned to the Ota'i for an afternoon swim and relaxation on a pool side lounger. That evening, as the sun was setting, I was treated to an *umu*, a traditional meal wrapped in banana leaves and baked in a stone-lined pit since early morning. It was a very special farewell night.

    The next morning I faced my seventh and last day on the island. After breakfast, the hotel van took me to the airport, where I was garlanded with a *rei pipipipi,* a necklace of local seashells to serve as a reminder—as if I could ever forget-of the very special experiences I'd had on Rapa Nui. Despite having trod and climbed and seen and touched so many of its riches, I was leaving with a feeling of not having grasped the full meaning of what I'd experienced. The enigma of Rapa Nui remained intact and I knew that the memories of my time on its nearly barren landscape would not leave me. Too soon I was looking down on the triangular configuration of that mysterious island set apart from other land, alone on the vastness of the Pacific Ocean.

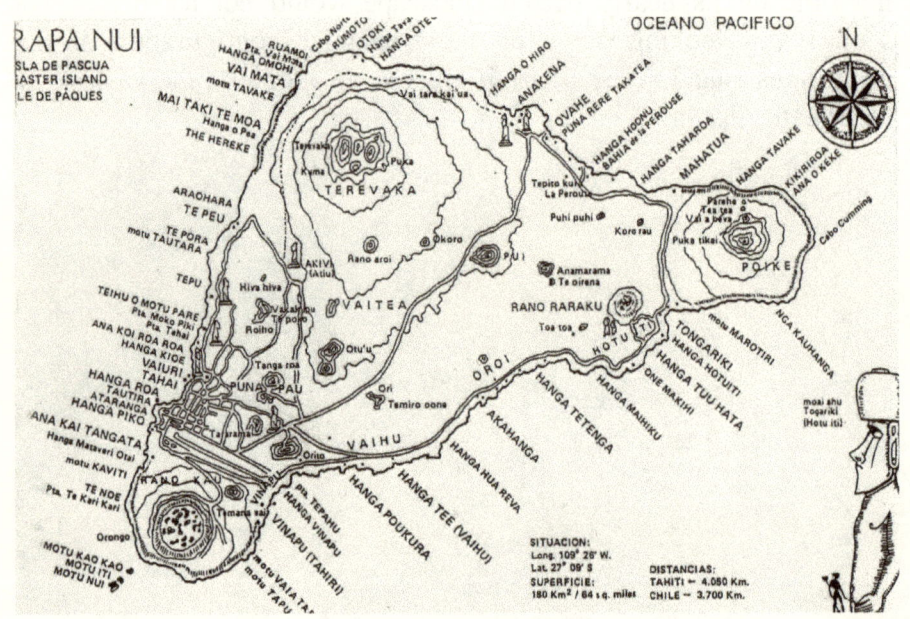

Map of Rapa Nui

THE
RITES
OF
STONE

EPIGRAPH

To say
I have walked
among the ruins,
been intimate with stone,
with sand, and the adobes
that have been preserved
. . . I have been one
in subtle colloquy with these,
witness to the rites of stone.

PART ONE

THE ANDEAN SUITE

CHANCAY

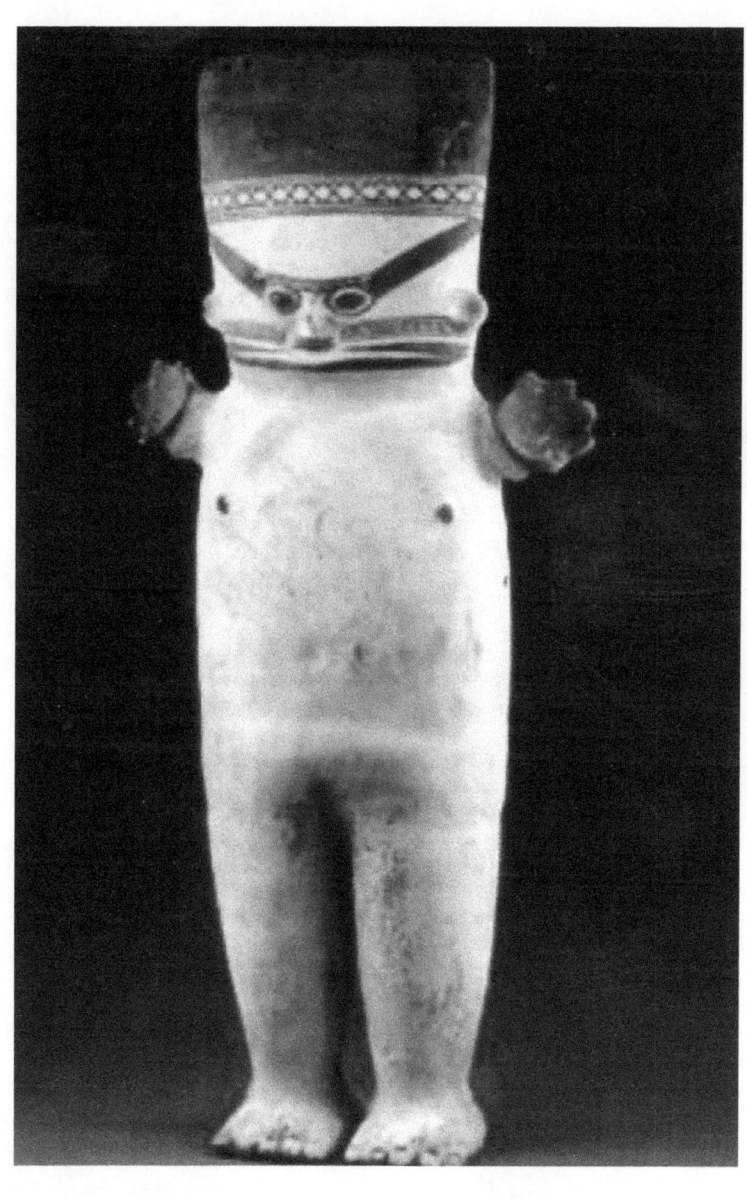

STILL LIFE

A walk among the detritus of centuries,
among the skulls and bones of death
that lie between the broken pots—
the shards of ancient lives.

Death heads caparisoned with hair
and ornaments of silver, copper, gold
enfolded in the woven cloth of burial rites.

For centuries the smell of death has lingered here,
still hangs on human parts and shrouds
which have survived the onslaughts of the wind
within the climate of the desert sands.

The site of past anatomies surveyed,
I've drunk the effervescence of the time
while sitting next to skulls with their patina,
and hanks of auburn hair on parchment skin.

The skulls that reek of death shout out
through broken teeth and trepanned lobes
the desecration of their graves and selves
to living bones among the Chancay dunes.

DUNESAYING

It is impossible to say
how best to recognize the living
in this valley of the dead.

The vultures overhead
must know the difference
that time makes.

CALENDAR

The hollow depth of skull
intent on introspection
in the coarseness of the sand

The cage of broken ribs
cipher of an inner state
scripted out of runic slants

The long perimeter of thighs
traced by sea-breeze
breaching foothills, sifting

The turn of knee-joints
on the curvilinear
of the unspliced shards

The dull fragility of bone
jagged on the edge of time

FILAMENTS

Cloth of ages
fragmented in past
functionless
except
in a non-sequitur
of memory

CHAVIN DE HUANTAR

CHAVIN DE HUANTAR

I

Sited where two spirals meet
within the interlocking hills . . .
matrix on the Mosna's banks

II

The stonewalled faces, tenon-heads,
rooted beneath cornices of sane design,
protrude with grotesque stare
and stoppered nostrils, incised cheeks . . .

Monsters strangely human in their mien,
suffering the task of bearing heavy walls
while nailed in the abyss of time.

III

The channels of stone temples—
passages beneath the skin of ruins,
arteries of life and death—
the secret shrines to cosmic gods
with lithic monuments of esoteric sense.

IV

Lanzón—
within the cruciform
of subterranean passages—
tapered, axial pillar
prismic in a triad of facets
looking toward the East,
cutting the earth
at the heart of the cross.

Stone in the Middle
which named this place.

Great Image
fanged, crescent-eyed, serpent-haired
with mouth that spirals into
Yin and Yang
strangely smiling in the darkness
until the solar ray bathes through
the channel on its side.

A tree within the underworld
with trunk of stone
[resembling life when it was
Center of the Universe]

THEORY

The genitals of gods,
their procreative function vast
[timeless, universal, indiscriminate]
and mystically obscure, heterodox,
must be in size, configuration
and insatiability
unlike the human counterpart.

Their metaphor, as in Chavín,
becomes the zoomorph or anthro-form
which graces, monstrously to eyes
unopened to the mystery of kennings,
the walls and stelae of
such ancient sites of cult.

CUSCO

SACSAYHUAMAN

Aerie scaled gigantically
between sky and Inka earth.

I

Cyclopean walls and parapets—
stones that zig-zag stilly
over ondulations of the hill—
protective and precarious
upon Cusco's brow.

II

The eagles, sated by thin air,
fill up the heavens with their wings
and, like the rendered stones
which form the walls below,
keep airy guard eternally
above the center of the world.

REMEMBERERS

strewing history upon expectant ears—
the past in gesture, intonation and
recall of total time,
too distant to have had identity

a data bank interned in primal hollows,
motifs brought up and out
to present time from sorties
into focal eye of mind

continuum to self's veracity

APACHETA

A pile of stones atop the hill
marks out in quaint geometry
the way that each who reached
had placed his burden
[symbolic in a stone]
upon the stones of those
who first confessed themselves
on heights in some antiquity
when sane psychiatry was art

RUNNER

Chasqui
is spirit
given the form
of
endurance

GARAGAY

FRIEZE

Inside the central monticule,
defining atrium wall with high reliefs
in ocher, blue, white, black and red,
the awesome curvatures and planes
of giant zoomorphic forms . . .

The image of a predatory beast
rampant on crustacean claws, insect legs,
with human teeth on elongated snout,
a crescent eye outlined in white,
a chevron back to feathered tail

A face in blue-gray puffed contours
more than profiled in fretted circularity,
both broached by curling glyph,
with tenuous fangs—fierce trinity
of white against ensanguined lips . . .

project themselves from beige perimeters
of the adobe wash once colored rose.

HUANCAYO ALTO—YANGAS

HUANCAYO ALTO - YANGAS

I

The furtive wrinkles on the brow of land
[narrowly caressing river banks]
which climb to steep, eroded heights
contain the stone corral, the granary,
the centers for a daily life
and burials beneath floors' domain
in houses with their facets
made of stone and layered mud . . .
the precinct where the coast and sierra merged,
as did the sacred and profane.

II

The hulks of cacti
jut across the rocky bounds
and press the hill for space
injecting thorny green
through remnant ruins
and crevices in stones.

III

Atop, the cacti and
the massive stones that shield
the terraces from falling rocks
purvey the silent history of time.

IV

Below
a cock crows
a dog barks

here, death
there, life
the one, decisive
its mark well made

the other, shabby
and without eternity

V

The fog sweeps in
too hurriedly
and all the habitations
of an early time
are soon secured
within the guardianship
of mist.

VI

The site dies on

HUARAZ

MONOLITHS

m

o

n

o

l

i

t

h

s

inscrutable in face

and in the grasping

of the hands

collected out of place—

within a garden

made of ruins—

alive in their strange discourse

of blank stares

FARDO

Sarcophagi are missing here.
Mummies are presented to eternity
bundled in the cloth of life.

PARTICIPANTS

Hollowness between bones

mummies
in a fetal pose
hands holding heads
in an eternal woe
as if the pain of dying
had not ceased
within the fatal context
of the grave

KOTOSH

KOTOSH

Hands that cross
upon the abdomen of wall
beneath the niche

pairs bespeak in clay
an antique body language
which implies: Touch Not
Prohibited and Do Not Profane
the sacred precinct, temple
of mysterious caste
buried in abandonment

LAMBAYEQUE

TÚCUME VIEJO

I

Cerro Purgatorio.

The Sun beats here
just short of Hell

II

Crenelated mounds
of earth and sand
commixed with shell debris
and remnant stone

III

Sea shells
offered once to deities
whose provenance was sea
are strewn about
the inland site
in a profusion
short of sand

IV

The mind soars with the condors
while the body crawls through crevices,
ashamed before the careless traipsing
of the blue-head, green-tail lizard

V

The dragonflies buzz endlessly.
Deranged birds let out howls nearby
while digging in the sand,
then fly a moment with a haughty grace

The fox and I, meanwhile,
traverse the pitted mounds,
each running scared, in his own way
to track the wild denouement
of this tactile place

Then, rhythmic waves of silence
carried on an unrelenting breeze
cross the avenue of death
beneath my eerie height

VI

Here, on the edge of sense,
there is a nuance
in the echo of Time

MACHU PICCHU

INTI

HUATANA

monumental

P

O

S

T

to which the
SUN
is hitched

secured
against
departure
to insure
fertility

sited
where the
GOD OF GOLD
attaches
Earth
upon the solstice
demonstrative of
potency

HUAYNA PICCHU

Breast of the World
shaped in the coil of stone
eroded, steep, vegetative
oozing forth the milk of mist

TAMPUTTOCO

Thrice
opened to the firmament,
windows into astral depths
defined through stones
in bold omission
to cohesiveness
between Earth and Sky

M O C H E—MOCHICA

MYTHOS

Chimor nobility descended from two stars
whose progeny, the Founder Taycanamo,
came ashore on a long raft, proclaiming:

> "The Great Lord sent me
> from across the Sea
> to govern Men and
> this whole Land."

And from Him came nine other Kings
who built nine palaces which served
as tombs for their remains as well as
those of whomsoever they possessed.

Their Souls ascended to the Sky
replenishing the pantheon of Gods
until the Inka conquered their domain.

VIRU

Clarity of Light.
The touch of timelessness
upon the temple's heights.

PALACE

I

Adobe site.
The ruins are so ancient
they resemble earth.

II

The sea borne on the breeze.
Precincts of once palaces
and tombs in brine.

III

The charge of centuries
through parapets
corrugated by the wind.

IV

Labyrinth of walls.
Unexpected turns eroded
by the elements.

V

Open eye for form.
The fish, the cormorant
enshrined on walls of mud.

OMISSION

Majestic in geometry, the lengthy, sweeping lines
define parameters of subtly abstract form
whose function and aesthetics are as one.

With bold incised designs on the adobe walls
of aviary species not discernible today,
with fish life and the products of the earth,

the ancient makers of this hollowed site
aligned the elements and made them theirs
within a scheme of magic in a sympathetic cast.

HUACA DEL DRAGON

The friezes
rich in implication
bold with myth
anthropomorphic

Adobe trapezoids
bespeak beliefs
of a primordial lineage
with raucous statements
rectilinear and curved
[the heads proferring
shapes of rainbows,
dragons with a serpentine
or fishtail form
extend their tongues
to each]

There once were creatures
such as these
when minds were open
to such miracles

CERRO BLANCO

Sun and Moon
wedded
by the expanse
of sand

separate
yet one

The White Mountain
witness
to their state in
space

PIECES

The coital actions
these ceramic pots declaim
with their mute strength
are ancient turns
preserving ways of life.

I

The penetrating penis
through anal venue of the mate
while she gives birth
assures the father's traits
will be enhanced within the child.

II

While nursing on her side
the anal proddings by her mate
will make the milk she gives
continue to convey his virile ways
to their male progeny.

The sympathetic nature
of coition's act
does not end merely with
the rampage of the flesh.

NAZCA

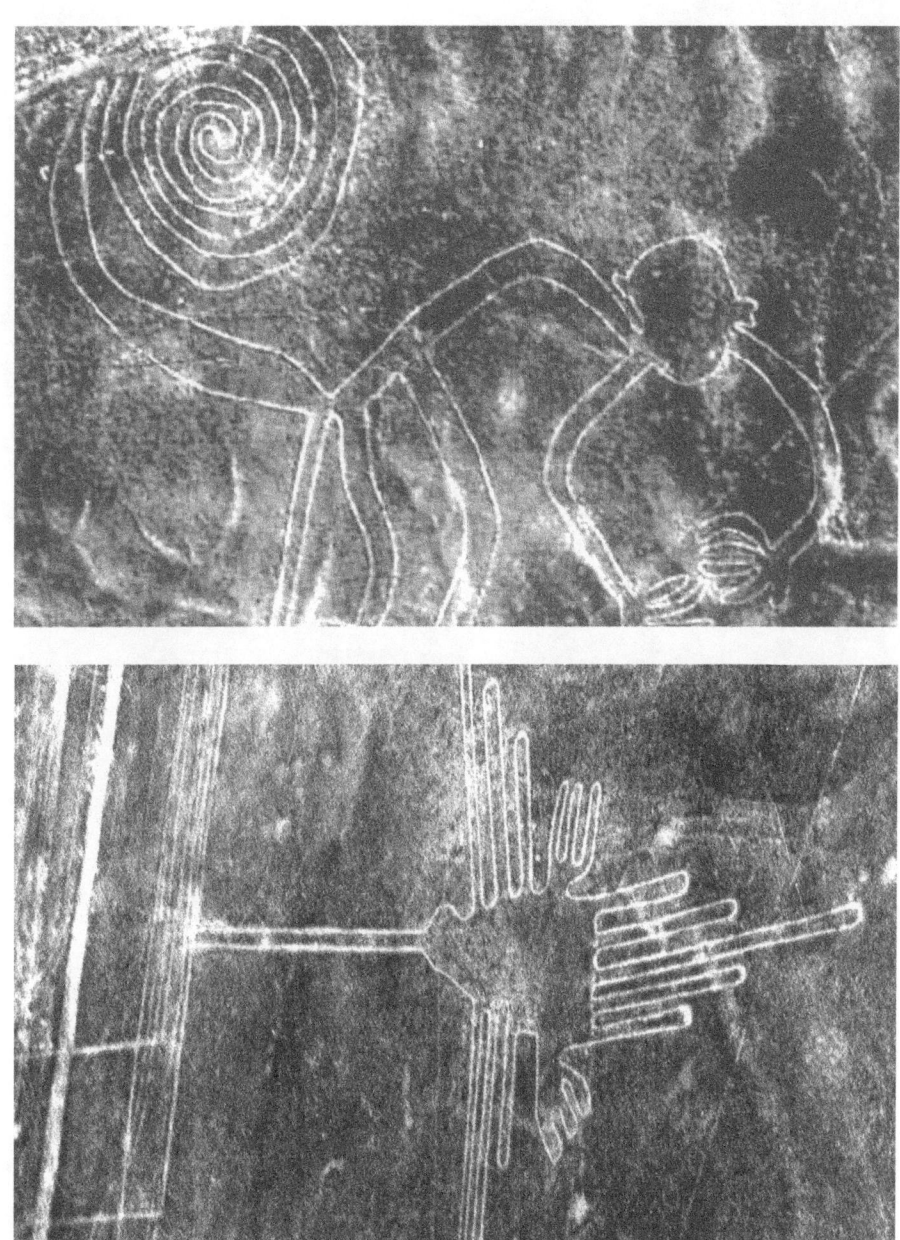

MARKERS

Disc emergent
over signs that point the way
from out the sands

lines, triangles and rectangles
of extensive lengths
surveying surgically
the pampa's breadth
with grave geometry
of astronomic cast

figures in the shape
of fiction's eye
designed by means
of occult art

surfaces give only aspects of the sense
the depth of barely-under-surface etchings
lies well beyond time's history

DESIGNATION

Intersections
on the concourse
of the plain

meaning drafted
with esoteric key
in lineals and spirals
frozen in the context
of impacted earth

OLLANTAYTAMBO

REMNANTS

Pink granite slabs
ripped haughtily from quarry walls
across the Valley of Yucay
then hauled in six asides
[movement secret in design]
to top the terraces of earth and stone,
enclosing mountain entrails
with monolithic mass
inscribed in stepping runes—
Ollantaytambo,
unfinished monumental work
above the Urubamba's rugged pace,
still guarding of the Cusco way.

LEGEND

The feudal noble Ollantay, a youth
who loved the princess of the realm,
had sought her hand in marriage from
the Emperor—her father and his lord.

But angered by the lesser noble's quest,
the Inka sent his daughter to be kept
secluded from unworthy eyes
within the Chosen Women's House.

When passion overcame good sense,
the noble Ollantay breached sacred walls
to hold Cusi Coyllur within his arms
throughout a night of love.

Discovered in the light of day,
he fled, returning to his bastion town
to raise his people up in arms
against the Inka's certain act of wrath.

Ollantaytambo bore the brunt of the attack
and could not be subdued outright,
but treachery achieved what might could not
and then the fortress walls gave way.

That day Lord Ollantay succumbed to death,
his blood upon the stones of terraced hills,
but Cusi Coyllur bought a child to light
and Ima Sumac bore the beauty of their love in name.

PACHACAMAC

PRECINCTS OF THE GOD

I

You can listen to the wind here
plying its ancient trade
over walls and earthenworks
never repeating itself

The sea, too, swells in on sand
with rhythmic variants
from strong to weak
in rounds of self-sufficiency

Before these premises beheld
the work of human hands
it had been so

Ever will be.

II

The stones live on
their dreams within
the hands that touch
i m a g i n i n g
the hands that worked
their profiles
to theologic heights
upon a time

III

The stones speak of

the nearby sea
which they can never reach
the sea which brought and took
anonymous migrations

the sea which in another age
may yet possess the ruins
and render unto stones
the homage of its rite

IV

The sea
the fertile land
the desert hills

The ruins oversee what once was theirs

V

The condor
circles high
above the sun

the minute life
clings on below
to fallen stone
with barely-green
tenacity

VI

The Mamacunas
raised the children then
where birds are now
sole residents
[within amphorae nests
that nestle in the ceiling's beams]

The species change but
life goes on protecting young
in its undaunted way

VII

The stones
lie on the whispers
of supremacy

YUNCAS

DEITY

PACHACAMAC

Maker of Earth
Shaper of Mankind
Impregnator of The Woman
Infanticide
Sacrificer of The Child
[whose meager flesh in burial
would turn to beans and gourds,
his supple bones to roots of manioc,
his minute teeth to golden maize
to fructify the World]

Creator
Healer
Killer
God

PAÑAMARCA

HUACA

beyond aesthetics
of stone and earth
summation

sacral mound,
uniting living ayllú,
extending ties to family
of the ancestral kin
within . . .

some also hold remains
of lesser memory
forfeited like adobes
plundered by the rain
and human hands

PETROGRAPHY

Geography of Stones

Circling Boulders
massive like whales
fixed in foreverness
in their plunge
out of earth

PARAMONGA

CITADEL

I

Lying on the land's inclines,
three structured terraces survey
the southern reaches of empire
with bastions, ramps and parapets.

Upon these, ceremonial chambers stand,
their stuccoed walls and niches primed
in yellow, white and red designs,
symbolic of purpose beyond might.

II

Through entrances and exits,
the wind continues touch
begun less earthily in past
when apertures were purposeful
and not mere means as now
for air's erosive work
or sand's tall penetration.

Thus, evermore, the plan of man
resembles nature's own incline of land.

III

Obscurity is what is left of function
in the distancing of centuries.

PURUCHUCO

DOMAIN

The scalpel of the unpaved road
dissects the fertile brown of just-sown fields
and barren mountain of eroding stone.

The massif stands, a sentinel above the site,
and nestles in the crescent of its rock
the ancient labyrinth of rooms, open to the sky.

Adobe maze which housed the whims
of some curaca, lord of all he viewed,
through angles measured with precision's gauge
and lines that charge the space without a swerve.

SECHIN

GLYPHS

There are no gods depicted in this art.
The warrior-kings stand glorified, majestic
on engraved stones that line the temple's broad perimeter.

Victors, bearing standards and the implements of war,
they oversee the casualties inflicted on their adversary's ranks
through mutilation as a way of ritual death . . .

visceras, decapitations, severed torsos, legs and arms
[crossed in pleading for protection from the blow?],
vertebrae and ears apart from proper linkages,

the flow of blood from eyes and neck and mouth and head,
the gritted teeth of pain on stones of anguish,
eyeless eyes dormant on the temple walls
[ironic in proximity to monoliths with eyeful stare].

The stone erected centrally before the bank of steps
exalts the stiff virility of a rampant warrior clan.

DECAPITATION

S e v e r i n g

with sharpened stone

the most unnerving, if
the quickest, way to
jagged death

a savage gravity
lurks within this ambiance
where severed heads are mimicked
on the upright temple slabs

SILLUSTANI

DEATH HEIGHT

I

The driving rain
tall upon the lake.
the red clay underfoot,
the often green or
sometime ochre mold
upon the moulded blocks
and on the boulders
strewn about the silence

II

Uneven stones
upright in patterns
of circular dimension
butting into hillsides
with their hard-cast edge

III

The chullpas rise suggestively
above the altiplano's height,
lithic monuments of death
stretched in rigor mortis
to the steel-grey sky

IV

The wasted lie against the stone
embraced by roundness
waiting for another birth,
perhaps the exit of some
longed-for resurrection day
when stones that open out of earth
will service an eternal need

V

Monuments to death,
erect like phalli,
cathartic to the living

CHULLPAS

The living, on the puna, had their days
within the humble frame of huts
constructed out of mud and thatch,
of which few have survived their time.

The dead were given ample shelter
from the temper of eternal night
inside tall tombs of fitted stones
which have endured in monumental style.

Ironic towers housed the dead of then
before the use of stone for living ends.

TIAWANAKU

PORTAL OF THE SUN

Within the scheme of rain—
the water irrigating ruins
and moisture coursing down
the channels of the Inti face
carved upon the upright gate—
there is an implication of tears

a dead god
living momentarily
only to decry
the terms of Time
in its long victory

or stoic deity
alive within the cryogenics
of the stone
awaiting the new vesting
by his cult
within a cyclical design

TEMPLATE

The Lord Creator, Sun,
beheld the disobedience
of some human progeny
and turned the lot to stone.

Within the inner sunken court,
embedded on the walls of stone,
the heads of men and women pose–
detached forever to proffer
the wonder and the pain
of witnesses to ageless equity.

PART TWO

THE PACIFIC SUITE

RAPA NUI

SETTLEMENT PATTERN

Hotu Matu'a
came from somewhere distant,
West or East,
vessels laden with his people,
crafts and lore,
landing at the Anakena site
of Rapa Nui's north.

Great Father that he was,
he founded there,
among palm trees and the sand,
amid volcanic peaks
and seaside caves,
the long-eared lineage
that would fast endure
beyond the reach of other hands.

But, late, disaster came.
The land was ravished of its trees,
the ancient mana was no more,
the great stone figures
once erect upon their ahu
were toppled from exalted heights,
topknots rolling on the ground,
coral eyes hurled to the sea,
as if Moai's relevance had passed
and other cults held sway.

*
* *

Rapa Nui still enfolds the mystery
of origins, of myths, of rites,
of its elusive fate:
it is arcanum
of an esoteric past.

MOAI

I

Statues in a rank
a frontal line
of singular dimension
near each to each
yet distant
in the fix
upon horizon's plane

II

They look through distance
over barren land
waiting for the second coming
face expectant
long ears listening
arms akimbo, hands to genitals
stoic in the silence of ages
eyes once with pupil of coral
and iris of scoria
mouth shut firm to pain
nostrils dilated
from breathing stone air

Humbled by time
which brings only the wind
to chafe the body
[pocked, discolored]
ultimately alone on a promontory
half buried in the navel of the world

waiting for the errant lands
to come together
as before the fissures and the sea

They are massive in expectation

III

Searching into night
the sky detaining
and releasing all at once
the flash of light
the long streaks dying
into birth
maneuvering velour night
r e s p l e n d e n t
with the radiance of raiments
out of space and timeless
and feet implanted on the lunar scape
crowned with muted heads—
landlocked lookouts
on an isle at sea

IV

The squandered heads fell tall
upon the grass-grown hills
and volcanic steppes of
silent, sea-seen isle

V

The long chance taken
the work unfinished
but evidence of dream erect
upon the landship's balustrades
majestic into eternity of stone

NIGHTFALL

At night
no light shines
beyond the shore.

A mass defined
by ocean on three sides,
the island
lies a bastion
to a prodding sea
that haunts
triadic shores
with dark caress

And its volcanos
do not light the night
with lava flows

At night
there is no respite
from the ink-dark sea.

THE LOSS

Irises were cast into the waters,
returned to coral reefs
from which they came.

Pupils made of scoria red,
deep with mana, wasted
on the life beneath the sea.

Moai stand,
their sight
unseen.

HOLLOWNESS

I

The sockets are blind,
the deep-set cavities
a hollow vacancy
on stolid faces
imagining
without sight

II

Form without function,
eyeless on the
wide expanse of land,
the tall Moai stand
bereft of vision
deprived of life

III

Yet at some times of day
the glow of sun
refracts from empty sockets
as if, by magic's stroke,
their mana were restored

RESTORATION

the red of life within
the white of death,

the few found eyes
entrenched anew
upon once vacant cavities
again empower statues
with the mana
of deific times

the ovoid eyes
look toward the land,
to the volcanic slopes
that nurtured them,
seeking people
out of past,
mutely asking they restore
the status and the rites
that once they had

sight restored,
absence nonetheless
p e r v a d e s
the tall Moai's stance

MAKE MAKE

The face of the Creator is a skull
or, as Orongo's bas-relief, all nose and eyes
atop the palisade that overlooks the sea,
across from Motu Nui and companion isles.

The site where sooty terns place nests
was given as a refuge to the migratory birds
but soon became a center for the Bird Man cult,
strangely honoring the god by raiding his preserve.

Intrepid swimmers from each clan would seek
the first-laid egg and one would rush the
intact treasure to the mainland cliffs
to then become the Bird Man for a year.

The Make Make image set upon the cliff
looked strangely stoic from his stone
on seeing that beside his own there was incised
the image of the man with birdlike head.

METAMORPHOSIS

His eyes are large
upon the birdlike face

His feet and hands
are in the human mold

anthropomorphic,
the Bird Man peers
across the water
from his bas-relief
upon Orongo's cliff
sighting
the islet
of his birth

ILLUMINATION

The island
is a deltoid
lacking
the interior
eye
that watches
and
illuminates

when eyes
of the Moai
are in place
once more
the light of
Make Make
will be
unified
and Rapa Nui
will become
Trinacria,
the Eye within
the Delta
casting
Light
across
the ages

ROBERT LIMA

is Professor Emeritus of Spanish and Comparative Literature, as well as Fellow Emeritus of the Institute for the Arts and Humanistic Studies, at The Pennsylvania State University. He has been named Distinguished Alumnus of Villanova University's College of Arts and Science. In 2003, His Majesty King Juan Carlos I dubbed him Knight Commander in the Order of Queen Isabel of Spain.

He is the author of twenty-six books of poetry, criticism, biography, bibliography and translation. Over four hundred of his own poems and versions of Hispanic poems have appeared worldwide, and over one hundred twenty-five of his articles have been published in professional venues. He has read poetry and lectured widely.

His poetry collections include *Fathoms* (1981), *The Olde Ground (1985), Mayaland (1992), Sardinia / Sardegna (2000), Tracking the Minotaur* (2003), and *The Pointing Bone* (2008), as well as several chapbooks.

He has been a Cintas Foundation Fellow in Poetry, Senior Fulbright Fellow to Perú, Commonwealth Speaker of the Pennsylvania Humanities Council, and is a member of the Poetry Society of America, PEN, the Academia Norteamericana de la Lengua Española, the Real Academia Española, and the Enxebre Orde da Vieira. He is listed in *Who's Who in the World, Who's Who in America*, and in creative writing directories in the U.S. and abroad.

The Poetic World of Robert Lima. A Retrospective, was an exhibit of his published poetry in books, journals, chapbooks, broadsides, and anthologies, together with others' poetry editions autographed for him by such poets as **Jorge Luis Borges, William Carlos Williams, Paul Engle, Denise Levertov, David Ignatow**, and **Diane Wakoski**, among many others, with whom he read in Greenwich Village and other areas. The exhibit was held at Pattee Library, The Pennsylvania State University, March 19—August 20, 2004.

In 2009, he won First Prize in the Phi Kappa Phi Poetry Competition for his poem "Astrals," which appeared in *Forum*, the international honorary society's journal.

http://www.personal.psu.edu/RXL2